Public Speaking Fear

Learn How to Beat the Fear of Public Speaking so That You Can Be Confident and Deliver the Speech Which Will Inspire Your Audience

By Clark Darsey

D1743765

Table of Contents

Thank you for purchasing this book and I hope that you will find it useful and helpful. If you will want to share your thoughts on this book, then you can do so by leaving a review on the Amazon page. It helps me out a lot.

If you enjoy this book, then you may want to check out some of my other books:

Self-Discipline Habits: Build Mental Toughness and Self-Control and Achieve Your Goals Consistently by Adopting Success Habits

Job Interview Questions and Answers: Winning Guide to Answering Even the Toughest Interview Question With Ease and Landing That Dream Job

Introduction

All human relationships are built upon effective language in speaking. Doors and opportunities open for people who know their way with words and who can speak well. Oral presentations are similar to any other human interaction with the scale being much, much larger. These kinds of events also have an effect on the relationships on a more intimate level.

A lot of people have a lot of anxiety when they only think of speaking in public. There is really no need for that and you can combat this easily. This kind of performance has been a part of our history for many centuries and it is held in pretty high regard by many.

Some people are excited by the possible challenge offered by public speaking while others don't even want to hear or think about having to give a speech. A lot of people have a lot of interest in getting over the fear of public speaking. Public speaking is among the most frightening things most people don't want to go through. The fear of public speaking takes the top spot, followed by a fear of death.

Even though speaking in front of an audience may be overwhelming, it is possible for a lot of people to overcome this fear. It is necessary to understand public speaking in order to be successful in overcoming this fear.

This book is all about describing public speaking so that you could understand and control your fears to a greater extent. After reading this book, you will be equipped with strategies that will make it more than possible for you to deliver a quality speech no matter if a speech is over video or on a stage during a special occasion.

Chapter 1: About Public Speaking

Public speaking refers to any talking that is done in front of a group of individuals. The size of the group doesn't really change the definition of public speaking. Whatever the case may be, this whole process is quite an ordeal for most folks.

Public speaking is an art form. There are no good speeches without crisp delivery that consist of pauses which emphasize what is important. Some people seem to be natural at this kind of performances while others can never seem to have their way with public speaking.

It is helpful if someone is naturally talented. Regardless, a person can become good at public speaking by being patient and practicing diligently. Knowing how to give an oral presentation can be learned if one knows what to do without getting discouraged. In order for a public speaking performance to be effective, it is necessary to have a certain structure and a purpose. Having a plan instead of winging it is what can make up for the lack of inherent talent and it is what separates pros from the amateurs.

There are a lot of reasons for public speaking occasions. Public speaking can be entertaining, for better or worse. Public speaking can also be informative and educational and it can have an influence on other people. It is necessary to have the purpose of the speech in mind in order to achieve a greater level of organization of thoughts and information.

Key Elements of Public Speaking

People can be very different based on the occasion and the context. People adapt to their environment. Before speaking in public, there are some things that need to be considered in order for the presentation to go well.

The first element of speaking in public is the individual who is delivering a particular speech. This person who is delivering a speech really has to think about how the speech will be perceived by the audience. What is really neat about public speaking is the fact that the speech can be personalized based on someone's presentation style.

The key element of public speaking is the message which is attempted to be conveyed. It is necessary to know clearly what kind of information is attempted to be presented. Good information is very important for any public speaking performance. A presentation which is well organized can make or break the whole event.

Another key element of public speaking is the method. The method can encompass many things such as the location where the speech will be held, prompts that would be used and so on.

The last element of public speaking is the reason why the speech is held in the first place. It is necessary to know whether the speech is of the informative kind or is it leaning more towards the entertainment side. Another possibility is in public speaking having the goal of influencing and motivating people.

Public Speaking Over the Years

Signs and traces of public speaking can be found in any civilization through history if one looks hard enough. There has always been a lot of value in the spoken word ever since people were around. Being able to communicate in this way is what has enabled humans to make as much progress as they have.

Communicating orally was the at the forefront until written communication saw the light of day. Thanks to the written communication, many valuable works were preserved so that future generations could benefit from them and find enjoyment in them.

Poetry was created as a necessity in order to make memorization that much easier. Stories and words would be much easier to commit to memory if they rhymed and this made it a lot easier for those who would go through with oral presentations.

Many civilizations over the history place importance upon the spoken word. No sphere of life could be separated from debating a discussing. Politics and religion are simply a byproduct of this.

Public Speaking in Today's World

Public speaking is very prevalent in a lot of aspects of our lives today. We are continuously informed and influenced by oral presentations. Spoken word is the main way of dealing with family and other people with whom we may want to connect with. It is possible to communicate with people on a global scale thanks to the massive advancements in the technology. Before, it would take a lot longer for word to reach its intended destination. Most messages can get from one end of the globe to the other instantly with the aid of the technology.

There are a lot of ways to go along with public speaking today and one example of this would be videoconferences. This way, the presenter can deliver a speech to many people without even coming in contact with the audience. It was never easier to communicate with the masses thanks to the rise of the communication technology.

Opportunities and Events

Telecommunications is what allows you to deliver your message although some people may find it weird speaking to something that doesn't provide them with any sort of feedback. Of course, there will always be opportunities where quality oral presentations will have to be delivered to a group of people right on the spot.

All events are different and some event may be of the informative nature. For example, it may be necessary to deliver a speech with the objective of warning people about the possible hazards in the workplace. If the speech is a good one, then a lot of people could be moved in a way which benefits you.

Some events could also be of the personal kind. For example, your friend may be getting married and the pressure could be placed upon you to deliver a great speech. It is necessary to be prepared in order for the message to get across successfully to the recipients, whoever they may be.

Chapter 2: Fears and Phobias

Merely thinking about delivering a speech in front of a group of people can overwhelm a person, but it is necessary to slow down and to remember the difference between fears and phobias. Things may be a bit more complicated than you simply being afraid of the task at hand. A phobia may be in question and if that is the case, then there are certain precautions that need to be taken care of.

Fear can be pretty heavy and overpowering, but it is necessary to be able to differentiate between the fear and the phobia. There are differences and similarities between the two and it is necessary to understand them in order to get to the best possible conclusion. If a phobia is in question, then a professional may need to be consulted.

About Fear

Fear is an emotion which is important and it does play a pretty crucial role. Fear exists in order to ensure that people stay out of trouble so that their chances of surviving would increase. It is all about self-preservation. Without fear, people would be doing dangerous things without a second thought. Survival of all people would be in question if fear didn't exist and fear is, therefore, good and we should be glad we have it.

Even though the explanation may be simple, fear is a bit more complicated and there are layers to it. Fear is a part of every human in order to ensure that they remain safe. Of course, people are different, and not everyone will feel the fear and anxiety to the same extent.

The body does react to the emotion of fear quite prominently. When people feel fear, they will feel the physical changes in their bodies. What truly happens is that autonomic nervous system gets fired up along with the activation of adrenal glands. People are very aware of the feeling of fear and how it feels physically. Most frequent symptoms are shaking, being tense and breathing rapidly. There is also a chance of faster heart rate, sweat and dry mouth as a result of fear. Blood is redirected from the brain towards other body parts which may have a greater need for the energy in order to tackle the challenge at hand.

This redirection of the blood flow from the brain towards the other parts of the body can be quite quick and some lightheadedness and dizziness could be experienced by some people as a consequence. The situations that make people fearful also tend to activate the fight or flight mechanism which mobilizes the person to either run away or to stand ground.

Only fears people are born with are the fear of falling and fear of loud noises. Any other fear is learned in some way. It is still unclear in the scientific community how helpful fear is as far as protecting people and to what extent are fears learnable. What is certain is the fact that the enviroment plays a role in the formation of fear.

About Phobias

Phobias are fears that are very specific and that are unreasonable in their magnitude to the point of being irrational. Phobias can easily be distinguished from regular fear by realizing that phobias are irrational and unreasonable given the circumstances. Phobias are actually a lot more common than you may think.

In some cases, phobias can be on the level of psychological disorders if it negatively impacts the ability of the person to go along with their everyday life in a satisfactory manner. For example, a phobia of dogs may not by itself warrant classification as a psychological disorder. However, such a phobia that would prevent a person from going into households that have a pet dog could be classified as a disorder.

Categories of Phobias

There are three categories of phobias which are recognized. The first category are simple phobias and those phobias are fears of things and situations which aren't rational. The second category of phobias are social phobias and those are unreasonable fears of social settings and occasions. The last category of phobias is agoraphobia which is the fear of not being able to get out of a certain situation.

Simple phobias can vary quite a bit and they can extend to all kinds of things and situations. Someone with this phobia wants to get away from certain things and situations as much as possible. The person with this phobia actually realizes the irrationality of it all and that is why those people don't necessarily always look for a treatment for their phobia.

Social phobias tend to be paralyzing to anyone who happens to suffer from them. Obviously, just thinking about public speaking would terrify a person dealing with this. The fear of public scrutiny would be way too paralyzing for someone suffering from this kind of phobia.

At first, agoraphobia was just considered to be a fear of wide open spaces. However, recent findings have indicated that the people who may be dealing with this don't want to leave the safety of their homes because they are afraid of finding themselves in a situation they can't get out of. Panic attacks are what can influence the development of agoraphobia since people don't want for those panic attacks to happen in an inconvenient situation.

All of these phobias are viewed as anxiety disorders. Possible treatment options for these conditions are cognitive behavioral therapy or medication. A combination of these two is also an option. Any other treatment option is likely a variant of cognitive behavioral therapy, such as gradual exposure to unpleasantness with the goal of desensitization.

Glossophobia

There are some important differences between phobias and fears. Fears are an essential part of our survival and self-preservation. As long as fears don't get out of control, they shouldn't interfere with the regular conduct of everyday life. On the other hand, phobias are over the top, irrational and excessive. There is a lot of anxiety when merely thinking about a situation which is the source of phobia. Phobia can impair an individual, unlike fear.

People that are afraid of public speaking may not be delighted with the fact that they have to go through with public speaking, but they can still do it even though they may not do everything perfectly. Such a person could lose their train of thought during a speech, but they would still manage to wrap it up successfully. There is nothing stopping this individual from going through with the public speaking performance.

However, someone who is dealing with glossophobia may not be able to do as well in a similar situation. Just thinking about public speaking would be enough for the paralyzing anxiety to ensue. To make things even worse, physical symptoms may also be present, such as nausea. People dealing with glossophobia avoid situations where they would have to address an audience like a plague.

There are physical reactions to glossophobia and those aren't too dissimilar from the fight or flight reaction. Fight or flight response consists of faster heart rate, a spike in blood pressure, rigidity in the muscles etc. Senses would also be heightened since the individual is expecting trouble, even though they don't feel like they could handle it due to the general feeling of lightheadedness. Fainting is also a possibility.

Certain people will try to speak in public and they will start exhibiting signs of speaking disorders which they never knew they had. They may also start to stutter and a bit more challenging words will tend to be difficult to articulate fluently. What used to be simple is hard, all of sudden.

Glossophobia is specific to public speaking. Some people may be suffering from this, but they may be able to mask it such as in situations like dancing and singing. One way to get over the anxiety of giving speeches is for the person to imagines themselves as an actor since that puts ideas of proactivity in someone's mind.

Chapter 3: Roots of Public Speaking Fear

The best way to get over a certain fear is to realize what is the root cause behind all of it. Fear is a crucial self-preserving emotion that protects us for the most part. It is one of those emotions that are a part of human DNA with the purpose of keeping us out of trouble. The fear of public speaking is rooted in self-preservation as well.

Fears are learnable since the only fears we are born with are the fear of falling and fear of loud noises. A certain fear can form based on someone's experiences. Interestingly enough, some people can develop fears by just seeing other people being afraid of something.

Everyone knows logically that there is no real threat during speaking in public. Still, some of the self-preserving emotions tend to get activated in these kinds of situations. Fear of public speaking isn't so simple since it combines our hardwired instincts with the fears which have been learned experientially.

Instinctual Fears

Public speaking is an overwhelming social scenario and there is a natural response to it. This reaction may actually have a purpose and it may be more than a mere annoyance. This reaction can be a form of self-preservation.

There are certain instinctual fears which are hardwired into humans. The purpose of these fears is to aid us so that we could make quality decisions under pressure so that we would stay out of trouble. Fear is a natural reaction even though it may not be pleasant for the body and the mind.

Fear is a form of a message which conveys that there is danger around. People are hardwired to be afraid of anything that can point to danger. High places are one example of something people are supposed to be afraid of. Our bodily reactions have to be strong so that we would realize that it is necessary to take action promptly.

Fear of public speaking is deeply ingrained in the human psyche and it seems that public speaking itself provides perfect conditions for this to be the case. It really shouldn't be surprising that the reaction to public speaking is such as it is since facing a whole crowd of people head-on isn't the most peaceful predicament to be in.

It is easy to get the fight or flight response activated if someone isn't prepared properly. A speaker probably knows on a logical level that the audience means no harm, but there still may be unease and an urge to seek some kind of protection. This is what makes this particular fear of public speaking universal to all people to some point.

Fears Which are Learned

A lot of fears can be learned through experience. Someone can learn to fear certain things and/or scenarios based on past experiences. A small child may not fear dogs at first until a certain experience teaches him otherwise. There are a lot of different experiences that can aid in the formation of fear.

Let's take dogs as an example, a child may learn to be afraid of motorcycles simply by observing someone else being visibly afraid of dogs. A child can also learn to fear dogs if an accident of some kind is witnessed from a distance, such as a dog bite.

Don't underestimate the power of the mind since it can have a large effect on most fears. Just imagining the experiences which tend to make someone fearful can be all that is necessary since a mind won't be able to tell the difference between the imagination and the real thing if the imagination is vivid enough.

How Does the Fear of Public Speaking Develop

There are not many people who will not be somewhat intimidated when they are faced with the task of public speaking. The fear of public speaking has its fair share of inherent fears. Some fears can be completely imaginary while others may be subtle and not so obvious. Everyone will have their own reasons why they feel anxiety about public speaking.

It is possible that some people may have had a traumatic experience when it comes to public speaking. Events such as these can have implications that can last a while. Only one bad experience related to public speaking can be all that it takes in order for someone to become afraid of speaking in front of groups of people.

A momentary fear that is intense enough can impact someone's whole life. Our nervous system simply works by associating fear with situations which could be bad and which should be avoided. The body will respond accordingly if anxiety and dread are felt during an event.

People naturally associate how they feel with what happened. Some people get the fear ingrained in them faster than others. Sometimes negative associations may not be connected with the act of public speaking in the slightest since a negative association could be formed just in someone's mind.

Most people learn to fear public speaking because of associations. It may be enough to be the witness of someone else's bad experience with public speaking in order for the bad associations to be formed. If the instance of public speaking is bad enough, then the observer will be weary of similar situations as well. A similar example would be a child learning to fear dogs because of witnessing someone else entirely getting bitten. Fear can be formed by just seeing the traumatizing event.

How Fear Builds Over Time

Fear of public speaking can also be developed over time little by little. An instance of stage fright which is very minor can evolve into something more serious if this accumulation is left unattended and ignored. The fear only grows stronger if someone focuses on it directly.

Very subtle experiences can compound into a fear which turns out to be overwhelming. The body overreacts since the response to the emotion of fear is too much alluring. If a mind belives something, then the body will do so as well and the feeling of anxiety can activate the nervous system.

The way in which fear compounds upon itself gradually can be explained by Pavlov's behavioral experiments. It is well known that Pavlov's dogs respond inappropriately to the bells being rung. It is actually a quite simple experiment. Just as dogs were about to be fed, the bells would be rung. It didn't take long for the dogs to start salivating when they merely hear the sound regardless if the food is served or not. The way their body would respond became tied with the sound of the bell.

There is a lot of power in associations. A mind can always make the experience seem worse than it actually is. Never forget that you are, for the most part, in the control of what you think and how you feel. You can rewire your body so that it responds differently to public speaking events and occasions.

Chapter 4: How Can You Unlearn Your Fears

Just as the associations to certain stimuli can be created, they can be unlearned as well if someone knows what to do. It is necessary to have the patience for this to be a success, but it is worth the effort. There are several ways in which reactions to things and situations can be relearned and rewired.

One way to unlearn your fears of public speaking is to adopt a cognitive approach. By doing this, you are deliberately using logic and rationality by constantly reminding yourself that the fear is not based in reality. It does require time to get used to working with emotions, but it is very possible to successfully adopt the cognitive approach by doing so.

A behavioral approach can also be utilized in order to change how you respond. Experts on behavioral psychology tend to refer to this approach as operant conditioning. Just as bad experiences can be anxiety provoking, the positive experiences can, in the same way, create pleasant feelings.

What you have to do is to keep reminding yourself that the fear of public speaking isn't based in reality and that there aren't any threats to your safety you should be worried about. Still, this kind of fear is pretty universal to people. The same feeling of fear and anxiety can be turned around into feelings of excitement and thrill.

You Can Unlearn the Fears You Have Learned

People use their set of beliefs as a guide through life. Some of those beliefs are factual while others are merely a product of faith. Some beliefs may be based on the perspective which is simply wrong.

Fear of public speaking is mostly rooted in a perspective that isn't based in reality and which doesn't make sense. Even though you may be anxious about public speaking, there may not be anything that would serve as a plausible explanation for those feelings. Most people who learn the fear of public speaking in front of crowds do so because of certain experiences and perceptions.

People stumble because of the way in which they perceive their audience. The audience isn't really a threat, but the person afraid of public speaking thinks otherwise. The nervous system is primed to respond to a certain fear if the mind and body come to the conclusion that there is a certain danger that justifies the reaction.

Only one traumatic event can cascade into phobias and fears for a lifetime even if the event itself was very brief. Just witnessing the event could be all that it takes. The good news is that someone can learn to be fearless again with some practice. Several positive events can be what is necessary to undo the damage of one bad event.

How to Gain Control

It is well known in a field of cognitive therapy that someone who takes a cognitive approach when dealing with a certain situation, makes an attempt to resolve an issue with a deliberate thought. In order to do this successfully, it is necessary to distance yourself from the emotions itself and this can be very fruitful even though it is not easy.

It is not easy to be objective and this is especially true when emotions are involved in the equation. Practice is required in order for the cognitive approach to work, but you can regain control of how you look at public speaking occasions.

What you think and what you feel is connected pretty tightly. You ultimately have control of what you think and you can use what you think to take control of what you feel. In order to rise above the anxiety and fear of public speaking, it is necessary to always be reminding yourself of certain facts about public speaking. There are no inherent dangers to public speaking. Your presentation doesn't have to be completely perfect. Everyone makes mistakes and they are a part of life. Whichever outcomes you are fearing are not realistic. The audience is not against you and it isn't out there to get you. You can't possibly control everything about the presentation.

Everyone will need to approach their fears differently since all people are different. A presentation contains different components and they all contain certain elements of fear for different people. You have to really think about which aspect of public speaking has the most effect on you so that you can cater your thoughts accordingly.

How to Change Your Response

Thoughts can be retrained and emotional responses to certain things and circumstances can also be changed. Desensitization is how reactions to fear can be minimized and this is at the core of exposure therapy which is all about gradually exposing a person to what that person is afraid of.

It is possible to get rid of the fear and a success rate is pretty high among people who commit to using strategies like desensitization and exposure therapy. In order to increase the chances of success and to save time, it is recommended to utilize these strategies intensively in a shorter period of time instead of doing the same thing over longer periods of time with lower intensity. It is necessary to be careful and to know how much intensity is enough in order to not make the fear even worse.

How Can You Desensetize Yourself to Fear

Esentially, desensitization and exposure therapy can be used by people to get over their fears. One way of doing this is to replace bad memories with positive ones. This can actually be quite simple and there is no need to overcomplicate things.

The memories of a certain fear reside within the region of the brain called the amygdala. When someone tries to control the emotion, that process starts in the region of the brain which is called medial prefrontal cortex which is the rational part of the brain and which sends signals to the amygdala and to the brain stem. Just like the fear response can be based in the amygdala, the feeling that a certain situation is safe can also be based within the amygdala.

People should be placed within the reach of new experiences that share the same source of fear with the thing they are persistently afraid of. It is possible to retrain the brain so that a person could relearn how to react to something in a more healthy manner. It is quite possible to instill the feeling of safety within the amygdala. When this is done successfully, the brain stem, which is a part of the brain responsible for automatic behavior such as beating of the heart and breathing, is also affected in a positive way since a person will be less likely to physically overreact by starting to breathe more shallowly, for example.

This is all possible by making sure that the slow and gradual exposure to the source of fear is accompanied by positive experiences so that positive associations would be formed. In the same way, people who are afraid of public speaking can get themselves exposed to very small doses of public speaking at first while also deriving some pleasure from the experience. If the experience turns out to be a pleasurable one, then this pleasantness is communicated by the medial prefrontal cortex to the brain stem and the amygdala. Bad memories in the brain can be replaced with more positive ones and this is how the reactions to fear responses are controlled.

There are people who swear that this whole process doesn't take more than a couple of hours while some other people suggest that a lot more time of someone exposing themselves to public speaking is necessary. At the end of the day, it all depends upon the individual.

Chapter 5: The Importance of the Audience

You should never underestimate the importance of audience in public speaking occasions. It is important to have a healthy understanding of the audience in order for the presentation to be a success. This can allow you to have a greater level of control over the crowd and to start establishing rapport if you manage to be empathetic enough.

This may seem overwhelming, but you should quickly come to the conclusion that the audience is your ally and that you should treat it so. A successful presentation can't be one sided. Using the visualization to portray the audience as an ally can provide someone with great public speaking success.

No matter which flaws someone may have with public speaking, they can be turned around and a person can become a public speaking star. It is all about knowing how to perform well in order to overcome the possible issues with articulation.

If you are sufficiently inspired, you can gain control over the situation in order to get the most out of the approach that would provide you, as an individual, with the best results. You can achieve what you set your mind to, whether that is to create a personality around your public speaking or to build rapport with your audience.

Your Audience Wants to Help You Succeed

Most of the anxiety that comes with public speaking can be traced to the faulty perception of the audience. If the audience is seen as the threat and as the enemy, then it can be very easy for the fear to develop. You will do a lot more good for your success if you reframe this and start thinking that the audience wants to see you succeed with the presentation.

Empathy is very important. Any member of your audience is likely to be weary of public speaking just like you are. The audience may be acutely aware of what you are going through and this can provide a presenter with a sense of calmness.

It is a fact that people like to see the demonstration of confidence. However, adding in some humor and humility can lift the presentation to a whole new level. Public speaking is an interactive kind of event. You should always keep in mind that the audience can overlook if you are not completely perfect with your public speaking, just like someone in a one on one conversation won't mind that much if you mess up a sentence.

You may think that a certain slip of the tongue or a stutter is a deal breaker, but it means barely anything to the people in the audience. It is the fact that you are your harshest critic and that you judge yourself way more than other people do. No one will criticize your presentation as much as you will.

Manage Your Expectations

It is not easy to manage your expectations as far as the audience is concerned. A person who happens to enjoy speaking in public may enjoy the task of public speaking itself since he or she understanding the importance of meeting the expectation of the audience.

When you are seeing a movie, the lines are delivered perfectly since they are rehearsed and practiced. The lines are rehearsed with the knowledge of what it is being expected and this is what makes it possible to deliver the line properly. Some people may be overwhelmed when they merely think of the expectations of the audience. Still, you can use these same expectations to get over your fear.

You can draw inspiration from the expectations of your audience. You should be aware of the purpose of your speech and about the information that your audience is expecting to get out of the whole occassion so that you could organize things properly. By being empathetic, you can assume the position of the audience in order to realize what are they expecting you to deliver on. You could also develop an understanding of whether you, as an audience member, would mind if the speaker made a slight mistake.

Motivation

Fear of public speaking can prevent a lot of people from going after what they want. You don't necessarily have to be very outgoing to be good at public speaking since there are many shy people who can do well with public speaking. Nature of the public speaking performance can be used to get over issues such as stuttering.

Some people may have a stuttering issue which is also preventing them from doing well in numerous social situations. There are ways in which this can be overcome by reading books aloud and working on the enunciation and articulation. This is a very simple approach, but doing it over the course of time can yield very impressive results in the public speaking department, even if a lot of people say that a certain individual would never amount to much in terms of public speaking. Such people actually tend to make the largest splash.

Don't Worry About the Control So Much

It is possible to rise above the challenges as long you really put your mind to getting better at public speaking. Some people worry about control and that is a huge hurdle for them. The act of public speaking is interactive, for the most part, but it is necessary to stop worrying about control so much in order to rise above the fear.

What you feel, other people feel as well. If you are feeling anxious, then you can be certain that other people will feel that. It may happen that some members of the audience are fidgeting which pretty much means that they aren't paying very close attention to the speech itself.

If you do not notice that some people fidget in this way, don't get diverted by that. You should maintain your focus on the things which you can control directly. If there are people who are giving off the signals of positivity, then try to feed off that energy. There will always be people who won't be all up in arms about the speech and it is necessary to accept this as an inevitability of the process.

How to Approach the Situation

Your approach is under your control. A strategy that is well put together can make or break certain speakers. Other speakers may prefer to play it by the ear without too much of a structure. Some people simply do better when they have notes while some like to keep the information contained in their mind since they find notes to be distracting and for those people notes can be a hindrance.

You need to be self-aware and have the knowledge of how you naturally interact with other people. If you are relaxed and spontaneous, then a short summary of the speech may work well for you since you find that you speak more naturally that way. Other people may prefer to have detailed plans and notes and that is perfectly fine. It is necessary to know what sort of approach will yield the best results for you specifically.

Whatever you do, you should always keep the audience in mind. Think about the speeches that have left a positive impression on you before. You can try to figure out what made those speeches so good so that you could mirror their success. You are naturally empathizing with the audience when you are doing things in this way.

Chapter 6: Tips & Tricks

It's never a bad idea to gather some tips and tricks about how to deal with the fear of public speaking. You can be more resourceful and you can work better with what you have this way. The best advice is usually very simple and very commonsensical. This sort of advice is easy to memorize and you can easily carry a reminder with those tips so that you never forget about them.

Everyone is different and therefore you will have to decide which tips will provide you with the best results personally. What may work great for you may not be as great for someone else. Just don't overthink things since you want to make taking the initial step as easy as you can.

How to Get Rid of Stress

Not being stressed is easier said than done and it is not actually entirely possible. What you should remember is that stress can be good. Instead of pushing against the stress, you can use it and benefit from it. It will take some time to assume this new perspective, but it will do you a lot of good if you can successfully adopt it.

You have probably heard countless times about the people who just tell you to not be stressed as if it were that easy. For most people, that simply doesn't work. The world would be a much happier place if it were so simple. Just focusing on stress can actually lead to anxiety since what you focus on expands.

Stress exists for a reason, just like fear. People need some stress to actually get anywhere. It is only necessary to worry if the burden of the stress becomes too overwhelming, and in that case, it is necessary to utilize certain techniques for managing and alleviating anxiety.

When you manage stress, you aren't letting it go. You can actually use it during your speech. If you know what to do with the release of stress, then you can end up bringing a lot of creativity to your speech.

How to Benefit from Nervous Energy

Stress should be looked at as energy which can be used in order to gain an advantage. You will find taking control of your anxiety to be very helpful and it will serve you a lot more than worrying about all the countless things which make you lose focus.

There are several ways in which this nervous energy can benefit you. By doing so you can create a personality around your public speaking which will allow you to deliver the message more effectively. For example, if you are not all that great at pausing and controlling the volume, then you can use the stress energy to focus on that.

You can improve your performance by knowing how to direct your nervous energy. As aways, some people will be naturals at this while others will need a bit more practice in order to accomplish the same thing.

You want to learn how to take advantage of stress instead of just letting it go. There is actually a great power there and it is a shame to let it go to waste just like that. Stress can serve a useful purpose and you can actually harness that energy. You can release the stress just by laughing. It is a lot better to use stress instead of just trying to rise above it. It is all about focusing on what you actually can control.

Be Aware of Your Limits

Everyone has their limits. You have to have good situational awareness if you plan to hold a presentation which will serve its purpose. A recommended way to deal with a public speaking occassion is to create realistic limits for yourself. You just have to keep reminding yourself that the audience is your ally and that they don't want to see you have a bad time since to them that is almost as bad as them having to deal with that themselves. In order to be within your limits, you want to make sure that your goals are reachable.

It is very good to have goals if you are using some form of exposure or desensitization therapy. It will be a lot easier for you if you have smaller milestones which should lead you to a large ultimate goal. It is way easier to learn anything if you can break it down into small manageable chunks. Your brain loves doing things that way. By just sticking to this process, you will learn a lot. You will recognize the fear and then you will be able to replace it with something a lot healthier.

Learning in small and manageable steps is a lot more realistic and manageable instead of taking huge leaps, regardless of the fact that taking huge leaps seems more glamorous. Everything is better than just jumping swiftly into a public speaking gig without having a strategy that is based on your limits. Just remember that huge goals can work against you and that realistic ones which you can achieve in your current state will work a lot better for you. Break down the whole undertaking of public speaking into small, manageable chunks first, you can make your goals larger later down the road.

Don't Get Stuck in Paralysis by Analysis

For anyone who is not a natural at public speaking, proper preparation is non-negotiable. Some people can naturally have hours of amazing stuff to say, but you don't need to go that far in order to get the job done as far as public speaking is concerned.

You shouldn't spend all your time preparing yourself since overdoing it with the rehearsing can work against you. You gotta realize that things are rarely going to play out perfectly and that distractions are always possible. Someone in the audience may not be on their best behavior, or you may lose your train of thought.

This is simply what you can expect when you are doing public speaking live. You could be sabotaging your chances of success by excessively preparing yourself for your public speaking event. You are aiming for perfection when you are rehearsing excessively and you may not be able to handle something unexpected. You should be ready for the unexpected.

You can also try to go way beyond your current level of capabilities when you overprepare. You may try to do too many things in not that much time which could result in blandness all across the board and you spreading yourself too thin.

Rehearsing is important, but it should be done in moderation. If you start thinking that you are overpreparing, then that is likely the case. You want to know which information in the presentation is essential and you want to stick to that instead of packing way too much filler in your presentation. Make sure that you really understand the material so that you wouldn't completely rely on memorization.

Chapter 7: Reliable Public Speaking Techniques

You Can't Go Wrong With Humor

Stress is released with laughter and anyone can benefit from that. You are not the only one under stress during the presentation, there is a chance that the audience is feeling quite similar. That is why it is necessary to create a warm, inclusive atmosphere which will lend itself well to some humor.

You don't need to be a stand-up comedian in order to make this work, it is enough if you use a bit of humor to harness your nervous energy in order to deliver it. You can't go wrong by adopting a lighthearted persona for the occasion.

You don't want to come across as trying too hard to be funny. Comedy is all about timing if you want to make it work well. You should design your whole approach so that the audience doesn't get the impression that they are in a comedy show. You don't have to go overboard, you just have to make sure that the presentation is warm and energetic and that there is an atmosphere of friendliness.

You can't possibly control entirely how your audience will respond and laughter shouldn't be your goal every time. What should be your focus is making sure that you and your audience are comfortable and this is done with smiling, eye contact and anything that would harness nervous energy in a productive manner.

How To Ensure That Everyone Gets What They Want

When you come across as a warm person who actually cares, you are making sure that both you and your audience win. There are a lot of things that tend to happen to every public speaker which would be viewed as an obstacle by most people. However, it is possible to take this obstacle and to turn them into an advantage.

One possible obstacle is the silent pause and this can cause many people to become anxious. It doesn't have to be that way. A pause which is intentional can do a lot for the presentation if someone knows how to time it. A good pause gives an audience an opportunity and a time to think about and to process what is being presented. The pause also gives you, as a presenter, an opportunity to figure out what is next.

Not every pause will happen perfectly according to plan and some will simply be a result of an accident. It is necessary not to panic and not to become paralyzed by fear which would only make this unnecessary pause harder to overcome. Some silence is inevitable and it is up to you how you will handle it.

If you want to have a method which you can use to get yourself out of the awkward scenario, you can simply repeat your last sentence with a stronger emphasis which should give you enough time to recollect so that you could move on. You can sprinkle some humor in order to shift the dynamic of the situation back to the positivity.

At the end of the day, you just have to remind yourself that nothing bad can happen and that there is nothing to worry about. The best thing to do is to see inconveniences such as silences as what they are, an opportunity to refocus and to move forward. You can create a scenario in which everyone can win by just learning to look at obstacles as opportunities.

How to Deal With Mistakes

Mistakes are unavoidable on the road to becoming a good public speaker. Only robots have a chance of doing things perfectly according to plan without mistakes, but people simply don't relate to robots. People will find it easier to relate if they see some flaws.

For example, a certain presenter may ask for a moment in order to recollect the thoughts. When the presenter regains control of the situation, then he or she can follow this up by thanking the audience for their patience and understanding. Something like this could be planned out as well, but it would make the presenter come across as more genuine either way.

As long as the presenter remains honest and warm during the presentation as a whole, the audience will barely register a slight mistake here and there. These situations can be really turned around by adding in some humor at such a moment.

The Power of Being Humble

People are universally drawn to the displays of humility. People in the audience actually want to relate to the speaker somewhat. An atmosphere of warmth and compassion aren't necessarily created by loud and pretentious personalities. However, this doesn't mean that anyone can just simply be themselves and call it a day.

You can form a personality specifically for your public speaking occasions. You don't necessarily have to reveal yourself as you truly are. This may sound manipulative, but most public speakers you admire actually create a personality specifically for their public speaking events.

Even if you have a lot of knowledge about a certain topic, it could still be a good idea to create a persona which would downplay that a knowledge a bit so that the whole situation would be more relatable to the audience unlike the situation involving a perfect, all-knowing presenter who never makes mistakes.

Purposeful Speaking

Your performance can be much better if there is a clear purpose behind it and if you believe in that purpose. The audience will pick up the fact that you don't really care about the information if that happens to be the case. You can make any topic engaging and interesting if there is a clear purpose behind it.

Your message should contain some value, but it can be hard to convey that if someone is way too caught up in worrying about their fears or about how they are being perceived. There won't be many issues you will have to worry about if there is a clear purpose behind the speech and if you are aware of that purpose.

It will be much easier to create a passion driven presentation when you have a clear purpose. It is necessary for a presentation to provide value before an attempt is made to inform or influence someone. Doing this can be difficult, but it can really pay off. For example, you may think that the reason for a holding a certain speech isn't significant enough. However, the speech itself is obviously important for some reason. If you can figure out that reason, you will find it much easier to create a value driven and purposeful presentation.

The Power of Focusing on Less

A little information, as long as it is selected carefully, can be really impactful. You rarely need to focus on more than a couple of key points which are backed up by evidence and filler.

When you are creating a presentation, you want to make it easier for the audience to commit key points to memory. It is the fact that people, in most cases, don't remember public speaking events entirely since processing auditory information can be overwhelming, especially if there is a lot of information. You always want to keep your purpose in mind so that you could keep the presentation concise. You don't need to have more than three or four key points in order to achieve this.

Your overall presentation can be negatively affected by too many information and details since that can create a burden. In the case of the audience being confused about the purpose of the presentation, they would have to sort through the information to separate the important from the unimportant and that is why it is helpful to have less key points.

You as a speaker will also be more stressed if you try to cram way too much information into a speech. Give yourself some space because by doing so you are allowing your audience to take in the information. Your audience will be more focused and will remember more if you make sure to have fewer key points.

Choosing the Right Words

Choosing the right words can really make a difference since that will add more soul to a speech. There is a lot of truth in this. You can't go wrong with clear and concise words which anyone can understand without ambiguity. Your audience will remember the presentation much more fondly if the content of the presentation is focused.

People don't like boring lectures and they will have a lot more appreciation for a brief delivery which has a good blend of pauses and emphasis. You are in the control of your key points and how you present them and your ability to do so well will have an impact on the experience of the audience.

How to Perceive Yourself

Your self-perception is something that is worth your attention. You don't want to consider yourself to be a public speaker because there isn't much use in comparing yourself to other presenters. You should develop your own style whether that means being authentic or having a persona specific to public speaking.

You don't necessarily have to be a public speaking star in order to get your point across effectively. The audience is something you should always be aware of so that you could deliver your message in the most effective way possible. You will just get discouraged by huge expectations if you perceive yourself as a public speaker since you will never feel like you are good enough.

The presentation should always be about the core purpose instead of being about yourself. You will just waste time and energy by worrying about how you are perceived by others since this is something you can't control directly. You should view yourself as a messenger with a role of getting an important message out to people.

Chapter 8: How to Gain Support

It will be very hard to rise above the fear of public speaking without having some kind of support from others. A lot of different groups of people can support you on your way to beating the fear of public speaking. Friends and family can help you a lot and there are also groups which are specifically designed to help people who deal with exactly the same fears and anxieties related to public speaking.

Just make sure that you are aware of all the options that you have at hand. Some people will get the best results through hypnosis. Other people will benefit more from a Toastmasters group. Taking part in public speaking classes can benefit you a lot. For the most people, working with friends and family to rise above the fear of public speaking will be the first choice.

Support From Friends and Family

A great way to get started with public speaking is to practice with a group of friends or with family. If you want to gradually expose yourself to the crowd, it is best to do so in a safe and controlled environment. This will take some practice, but you will inevitably become more comfortable with public speaking if you keep at it.

That is essentially what exposure therapy and desensitization are all about. It is about making you realize that you are safe. The practice is much easier if you don't have to concern yourself with judgment. Try to be less of a perfectionist in order to reduce some pressure from the whole situation.

Take your time when choosing your audience. This will work the best if your friends and family provide you with honest feedback and they will do so as long as they are interested in you succeeding. This is how you find out if you know how to speak with purpose. Good feedback should address the key points of your presentation.

Public Speaking Courses

Not everyone will be thrilled with the prospect of taking a public speaking class and they may prefer going to a dentist over a public speaking class. The fact is that the same people who take these classes have the same fear and anxiety as you do. If someone can rise above these fears, then a lot can be gained from these classes.

Public speaking classes can provide you with all kinds of techniques you can use to improve your speeches and your confidence overall. These techniques can also help you get over your fear.

The best approach is to focus on the purpose of the speech and the techniques instead of how you are being perceived by others. There is a personalized element to these classes and you can be helped with finding out which approach will provide you with the best results. The right choice of approach will ensure that you can keep your composure and not get emotional.

Using Hypnosis

Another tool you could benefit from is hypnosis. Fears are ingrained deeply into how you think and how you physically react during fearful circumstances. Hypnosis can make overcoming the fear of public speaking that much quicker and it can act as a shortcut.

However, not everyone requires hypnosis and whether it is necessary, should be decided by a health care professional. Most common hypnosis techniques which could be utilized by professionals are visualization and relaxation. If someone can't let go of their fears, then those approaches are a good idea.

Toastmasters

It won't be easy to find a better resource than Toastmasters International for getting over the fear of public speaking. The Organization features numerous services and support which have the ultimate purpose of helping you get over the fear of public speaking.

Everyone is different and that is why a lot of information and resources are tailored towards individual's s specific needs. It's hard to not get something out of Toastmasters International. Even those who don't necessarily have to deal with the fear of public speaking can gain something from what is offered by Toastmasters.

The information which is provided can range from tips for beginners to inspiring stories which can help you get over your fears. The organization creates an atmosphere of belonging for everyone, no matter where they may be in terms of their speaking abilities.

Chapter 9: How to Get Started

It can be a lot easier to overcome the anxiety of speaking in public if you are aware of what fear of public speaking entails. It really helps if you are aware of the severity of your fear before getting started. You can start taking action once you are aware of where you are with your fear.

You need to know how to evaluate your needs in order to succeed. Some people may benefit more from a cognitive approach while others may need to consult a professional such as a physician or a hypnotist. You are not alone when it comes to the fear of public speaking. A lot of people are dealing with the same thing when it comes to how they react emotionally and physically. There are a lot of good reasons for taking action in handling the fear of public speaking. There are also a whole lot of stories which can be used for inspiration and encouragement.

Most importantly of all, you have to apply the theory since knowledge is only potential power. Just knowing what to do isn't enough. You will get over your fears as long as you regularly apply the techniques and approaches. An approach you will undertake should be tailored to you specifically.

Fears and Phobias

Fear is a natural response to certain things and circumstances and it plays an important role in making self-preservation possible for people. It may seem like the fear of public speaking doesn't make sense, but it isn't so unreasonable when you consider how it may feel standing and facing the crowd head-on.

A phobia is a fear which is excessive and which can prevent a person to go about everyday life normally. Some people may have a phobia of speaking in public, which is also referred to as glossophobia, and this may be behind some of the other fear of that person.

Know What You Are Dealing With

Fear is a strong emotion and it may be tricky to figure out if someone is dealing with a simple case of stage fright or if glossophobia is in question. There are ways in which you can determine the severity of your condition.

If you are finding it difficult to go normally through your day without being anxious about a chance of speaking in public, then it may be recommended to consult a professional. Phobias can be treated very effectively and the treatment can surpass someone's expectation with how well it works.

Know What You Need

Everyone's situation is different since everyone has different experiences and memories which means that the extent to which people are scared varies. The best approach is to start small and simple and to visualize your speech in front of a small group of people. Pay attention to whether that scenario is easy or overwhelming for you.

Some people may require a professional approach such as therapy while some will use medications if their situation is more severe. Certain medicines can effectively inhibit how someone responds to fear so that the situation could be handled in a more controlled manner.

Other people may find that utilizing a cognitive approach could help them be more rational towards public speaking instead of being emotional. Others may benefit the most by collaborating with other people in a public speaking class or with some other group such as family and friends.

For most people, Toastmasters International can be a great resource to deal with the fear of speaking in public. Toastmasters organizations is all about helping people with this fear and this fear specifically.

A Universal Issue

Bravery isn't the absence of fear. Bravery lies in the ability to overcome fears. There aren't many people who don't feel the fear of public speaking. This feeling is pretty natural and to be brave, you have to know how to control this fear.

Reactions to Public Speaking

Emotional and bodily responses to speaking in public aren't anything unnatural although the extent of the reaction varies from individual to individual. Some reactions such as dry mouth and shallow breathing can be expected as a part of the public speaking experience. These reactions will be there most of the time and it would be useful to know how to use them.

All of those reactions are a form of energy and that energy can be channeled positively as you deliver your speech. This nervous energy can be your tool if you know what to do with it.

The Audience is Your Friend

The fear of public speaking simply comes with being human and that is why some sympathy can be expected from an audience every time you are in a public speaking situation. Almost anyone can relate to this fear, and that is why it is helpful to view the audience as an ally instead of viewing it as an obstacle.

There is a reason why your audience is attending a speech. A speech has to have a purpose. Fears tend to diminish when the focus is placed on what an audience needs and why they are there.

In order to work better with your audience, you could include some humor and humility into the presentation. The audience is likely to be aware of your fear about the whole situation and the fact that simply going through with the speech requires bravery. If you see certain audience members return to following speeches, then you know you are doing something right.

How you perceive yourself and the situation is powerful. If someone goes into public speaking thinking that they have to have extraordinary talent and wits, then they are more likely to suffer from overwhelm. The easy self-perception tip to follow is to see yourself as a purpose driven individual.

There is an invisible flow of energy between the presenter and the audience. Things that tend to make people nervous can be turned around in the speaker's favor if fear is recognized as excitement. Recognizing that the speaker and the audience are in the whole thing together really helps.

Conclusion

The fear of public speaking can be overcome by reengineering your perception of yourself. The ideal way to perceive yourself is a crucial part of the audience instead of as a speaker who is facing an audience. A speaker acts as an extension of what the audience is hoping to get out of the presentation.

In order to get over any fear, practice is necessary. Which approach will be utilized will depend on the severity of the fear. Everyone has uniques experiences and the best results will be gained by adopting an approached which is personalized towards an individual.

Just having the knowledge isn't enough and just sitting on that knowledge will produce little in terms of results. It requires action to apply the knowledge after the ideal course of action was established for the individual.

It's best to start off small and it is best to start the practical application with something as simple as imagining giving a speech to the audience. The size of the audience can be whichever size someone is comfortable with. Someone can easily determine if they are dealing with a fear or a phobia by taking the first step such as this one.

The framing of the situation changes how the situation is seen. If someone can see the situation for what it is, then it is easier to approach a task in an objective manner by adopting a cognitive approach. This can only be successfully achieved through practice and through a commitment to mastering the responses towards public speaking.

An easy way to practice speaking is to have one idea which the speech is centered around. Getting the point across clearly should be the main goal. You can also practice by utilizing pauses to add emphasis since you won't do as well with speeches by trying to fill every second with speaking and not embracing the silence.

In order to be objective successfully, it is necessary to understand the origin of the fear within the brain. The brain is wired for the body to react automatically to certain stimuli. It is necessary to look at these responses objectively and to accept that they are the part of the whole ordeal.

To really get a grip on your fear, make sure to use the tools and resources that are already at your disposal. Groups can be used, such as Toastmasters, in order to get good personalized information and a sense of belonging. Friends and family can also be used for support as long as they remain open and honest with how they react. Practicing in a safe environment around people who want to see you succeed is how you get to the root of your fear.

If it turns out that glossophobia is the real issue, then a professional should be consulted. Techniques and methods such as desensitization and exposure therapy can be used to help with that. Some people may benefit from hypnosis since the brain is rewired to respond to public speaking environment and situations in a healthier manner. Successful hypnosis can make the whole process go much quicker.

If you want to see progress, then you need a plan of action. If there is something you want to overcome, such as a stutter, then you need to dedicate yourself to the process of turning that around. You can overcome the fear of public speaking by practicing speaking about a topic you are passionate about, whatever that may be. You will always do better if you talk about your interests. This is only the beginning, presentations which are interesting no matter the subject can be created by someone skilled enough.

In order to attain the skill, it is necessary to practice, and practice comes in many variants. One example is reciting parts of your favorite book in a place where you are out of reach and where you won't be interrupted. To practice effectively, it is necessary to channel the nervous energy in positive ways. Practicing like this over time in combination with relaxation techniques will produce great results.

Some stress is to be expected when delivering a speech. The response to the stress is what is most important. Relaxation techniques will be different for each individual. The right approach for you is the one which will provide you with the perfect balance between anxiety and good performance. The audience can be imagined as a group of people who are there for good information. Doing this takes some pressure of the whole situation since you are positioning yourself merely as a messenger.

In order to succeed, it is important to familiarize yourself with the process. Practice does make perfect when it comes to public speaking. Whenever you do anything for the first time, it is unlikely to end up being great. Sometimes the task can be completed easily without much effort while in other cases you can struggle with no end in sight. No matter how much effort is required, tasks can be mastered if someone is persistent enough.

It is necessary to keep reminding yourself that it is possible to overcome the fear of public speaking and that the only thing that differentiates someone starting out and someone with inherent talent is the time it will take to reach the goal and the willingness to keep going. It all comes down to willingness since just because someone is talented, that doesn't mean that the person will do what it takes to reach their goal.

I hope that you have enjoyed this book and that you will find it useful. If you want to share your thoughts on this book, you can do so by leaving a review on the Amazon page. Have a great rest of the day!

Printed in Great Britain
by Amazon